The Right Way
By

Jeffrey Erickson

Jeffrey Erickson

Copyright © 2018 Jeffrey Erickson

ISBN-13: 978-1731548726

Prologue

In 1964, there was a unique event in an NFL game that many still call the biggest blooper ever. The Minnesota Vikings were playing the San Francisco 49ers, and the game was in the fourth quarter. San Francisco had the ball, and the quarterback threw a pass to Billy Kilmer, who caught it and was fighting for extra yards when he fumbled the ball. The Vikings defensive end, Jim Marshall, picked up the fumble and somehow got turned around. He then raced for the end zone and crossed the goal line nearly 70 yards later, untouched. Jim was so excited about his fumble recovery and lengthy run for an apparent touchdown that he threw the ball toward the stands. The problem for Jim was that he had run the wrong way into his own end zone. Instead of scoring a critical touchdown for his team, he had scored a safety for the opponents. Traveling in the wrong direction did not bring the positive results that Jim had anticipated and hoped for and had even begun to celebrate.

In life, there are many directions we can travel, many destinations we can set our sights on, many roads we can choose. There are rocky roads, roads with ruts, smooth roads and dead-end roads. There are "strange roads," roads less traveled, familiar roads and long and winding roads.

And, then, there is "God's road." God's road is the "right road," it's the only road that leads to lasting joy. It's the one road, the only road that leads back to our heavenly "home" and, ultimately, to eternal safety and rest for ourselves and our families.

Yet, as the scriptures tell us, when it comes to God's road, *"few there be that find it" (Matthew 7:14).*

Like Jim Marshall, many of us, even many of us who profess to be on the right path, are actually traveling in the opposite direction, moving under our own power, and going completely the wrong way.

Even worse, all the while, in our delusion, we often are celebrating—and all for the wrong reasons, all with the wrong map in hand and the wrong goal in mind. Oh, how wrong this wrong road thinking is!

We've been told to: *"Enter ye in at the strait gate: for wide is the gate, and broad is the way, that leadeth to destruction, and many there be which go in there at:*

Because strait is the gate, and narrow is the way, which leadeth unto life ..." (Matt. 7:13–14).

We've been invited, even commanded, to enter and to follow the right way and, we have been promised that by so doing we will have life—life everlasting, in fact.

So, just how do we go about avoiding the destruction that comes from following the wide and broad way? How do we avoid scoring a safety and, instead, score for our own team, advance our own progress, and win our own eternal salvation? Most importantly, how do we find and travel the path that will lead us to happiness now and to sheer and total joy everlastingly?

In this book, I will attempt to point out what God has designed for us in His great and merciful plan. I will try to show what the right way is, how to search for it, how to find the answers, how to discern His ways and, in the end, how to find the right and only way to God and into His presence. I pray you will enjoy the experience as you read, and ultimately find and follow *The Right Way*.

Dedication

To my mother Carol, who as a teenager diligently searched and found the right way. Her decision to ask of God and act accordingly has blessed my life ever since.

Table of Contents

The Right Way

Last year we built a new house and, as we began, we quickly found there were plenty of decisions to be made. We had to choose the type and color of everything from hallway floors, to carpet for the bedrooms and tile for the bathrooms. We had to make decisions about overall square footage and the number of bedrooms and bathrooms. We had to select the kind of windows and doors we liked, the color and style of cabinets, appliances, lights, and faucets. We even had to choose what to do for landscaping, what trees and bushes we liked and whether to have rock or grass in the yard.

Truthfully, the decisions were endless, and, for each of those choices, there were far more options than imaginable.

The toughest decision of all might have been paint color. When you walk into a paint store, you are hit with an array of thousands of color chips and then, if you don't see a color you want on a chip, you learn you can have a color mixed, so you have an almost infinite number of color choices.

How does someone ever settle on one color when there are so many choices?

When it comes to religion, values, beliefs, morals, ideals and standards, the choices are nearly as many and as varied as paint colors.

However, unlike paint color, and unlike the myriad of other choices we face in life, this most important choice isn't left to us alone. God has directed what the "right" color is.

While the options seem endless, when it comes to religious beliefs and values, God has outlined for us the right way. He has pointed out THE truth, the light and the one way that we should live.

And, yet, as we have already established, "few there be that find it."

Some of our wandering stems from the fact that God's way, the right way, is unlike the many other paths in the world.

God reminded us, *"For my thoughts are not your thoughts, neither are your ways my ways, saith the Lord. For as the heavens are higher than the earth, so are my ways higher than your ways, and my thoughts than your thoughts" (Isaiah 55:8-9).*

The Right And Only Way

Over the past few years, I have read about a handful of tragedies that have occurred on roads where someone was driving the wrong way or a different way than they were supposed to. Among those was the story of a young college student who had been drinking and jumped into his car.

He headed north onto the freeway in his Jeep Cherokee. The problem was, he was traveling on freeway lanes that were to be driven south. His choosing the wrong way

14

ended in tragedy, as he hit another vehicle that was heading southbound.

The vehicle he hit exploded and two adults and one child died in the accident.

This tremendous wrong-way tragedy will now negatively impact the rest of his life and the lives of many others as well.

I am certain if we interviewed this young student today and asked him if he regretted his poor and "impaired decision" to go the "wrong way" that night, he would emphatically say, "Every day of my life!" ("UNC student charged in fatal I-85 wrong-way collision," July 20, 2015. Accessed at: WRAL.com)

Going the wrong way on a road leads to heartbreaking events, tragic consequences and poor outcomes—and these negative consequences are even more devastating when traveling the wrong way in life. Sadly, even when we know the right road, we sometimes fail to follow it.

In the summer of 1982, a PSA flight from Los Angeles to San Diego was getting ready to land, when air traffic control warned them of a small Cessna in the area. The PSA pilots had seen it, but, for a few minutes, lost eye contact with it.

On approach, air traffic control reminded them again about the Cessna. The crew thought they had seen it on the left, or in what is referred to as the "nine o'clock" position; so, they dismissed the potential danger.

They ignored the warning and proceeded on "their" path. Suddenly, on descent, there was a thunderous noise as they hit the ascending Cessna directly beneath them. In a moment, the huge commercial plane was on fire and descending at 300 miles per hour out of the sky.

The plane hit the ground, killing every one of the passengers and a handful of people on the ground as well. Why? Somehow the crew had just stopped paying attention to details along their path that mattered, while they were flying. It was their job to keep the passengers safe. It was their job, with the help of air traffic control, to govern the air space around them.

As a crew, they had flown hundreds of times; they somehow became complacent, ignored the warnings, and passively dismissed the dangers around them.

We cannot dismiss the truth about God. It matters. It is important. We must pay attention to the path and direction we are traveling. We must pay attention to eternal things, as they are the things that matter most. Our eternal life depends on it.

The scriptures appropriately call the right road the strait and narrow path or the "right way." The right way is the only safe way, it is the only sure way, and it is the only true way to happiness, peace and joy. It is the only way where you can be assured you are traveling the proper course to a celestial destination in the kingdom of God.

Elder Richard G. Scott shared a powerful story about a nuclear submarine in its last phase of shakedown trials. Shakedown trials include an intense series of tests to make sure a submarine has been manufactured according to specifications and that it is safe and ready to be delivered to the Navy.

In this particular case, when the testing was almost over, the submarine was as deep as it could go and traveling at flank speed, which means it was advancing as fast as it could go in the water.

The helmsman, noting a slight upturn, took measures to right the sub by tilting the bow planes downward. Just as he did, the submarine experienced a total power failure. This meant the sub, still at flank speed, was now locked in a downward dive, going deeper and deeper. Without power, there was no way to correct the planes. Members of the crew knew that in moments they would be at a depth that would crush the submarine's hull and their lives would be lost. Panic ensued.

One petty officer, however, was calm. He immediately dropped to the engine room floor and began pulling himself along the floor. He got to a cabinet, reached in and turned a switch that activated an alternative power supply, and, thus, not only saved the submarine, but preserved the lives of all the crew members aboard.

How did he know to do this? In prototype school, they had done this exercise time and time again. He had been trained on exactly what he should do in the dark when the power went out. (Richard G. Scott, 21 Principles, Deseret Book, Salt Lake City, 2013, p. 50-51)

The petty officer had been trained in "the right way" for this situation, so he knew exactly what to do. He followed the plan and the pathway to perfection. In the darkness, without physical vision, he still knew the right way that led to a specific destination and a life-saving solution. His precise execution and exactness in following that path saved the entire crew.

As mortals, we may often believe we are "in the dark" when it comes to God's way.

The world has five major religions, an estimated 4,200 additional religions, and millions more personal views, ideas and beliefs.

Yet, despite the veil of forgetfulness we experience at birth and the darkness and confusion of the world, God has a perfect plan, including the means and assistance to help us find and follow that perfect plan.

God reminded us in our day:

"For there are many yet on the earth among all sects, parties, and denominations, who are blinded by the subtle craftiness of men, whereby they lie in wait to deceive, and who are only kept from the truth because they know not where to find it—" (D&C 123:12).

King David teaches us that *"God has His ways, statutes, laws, mercies, judgements, His word, precepts, way of truth, testimonies and commandments (Psalms 119:1-41).*

Jacob reminded us of *"the strictness of the word of God" (Jacob 2:35).*

These specific scriptures don't speak of a God who doesn't care what we do, what we believe or how we live. Instead, these thoughts affirm that God is specific, definitive, detailed, and particular about His children, His earth and His plan. For those who say God doesn't care what we believe: Even on the surface, that idea seems to violate everything about God's character, actions, approach, plan and purpose. We are His children, and He does care.

When we do things "the right way," or God's way, things will work out because God has promised they will. He has promised that His way is the "only way" to peace,

happiness, personal contentment and eternal
life.

Finding the Right Way

A few years ago, I was at Zion National Park in Utah with a few other Boy Scout leaders and some priests (sixteen- to eighteen-year-old young men) from our ward (congregation).

One of the day-hikes we planned was a 12-mile, beautiful, very challenging and rewarding hike called "The Subway." On the subway hike, at one critical juncture, hikers descend 400 feet to the canyon floor. There is only "one way" or one point of descent, and if you cannot find this exact path, you are stuck on the top of a 400-foot mountain platform that extends for miles.

I had been on that hike twice before, but only once from the top down, which was the way we would be hiking the canyon this time. I was to be the guide for the group.

In preparation, I printed out some information that I figured would serve as a form of map. The printed material and my faded memory of the hike, I assumed would help me find the correct path and the right way down the mountain.

We started the hike, and everything was going as planned, for a time. After we had hiked for some time, I thought we should have arrived at the critical point of descent to the canyon floor, but we couldn't find it. I knew if we didn't find this critical juncture soon, we would have to turn back.

With the young men following me, I tried a few different routes. All of the routes failed. At one point, I thought we had gone too far, then I thought we had not gone far enough, then I tried a route that took us to the edge of the 400-foot drop. We went forward, then backward, and then sideways. I was essentially leading our group in circles. I just could not find the right path.

The other leaders also tried and were unsuccessful in finding the correct trail. After some frustration and feeling very lost, we finally called our group together, and we had a prayer. Tyler Danielson, our Young Men's president, said the prayer, and he asked God to bless me (the lost guide) that I might be inspired to find the path down. When the prayer ended, I unfortunately still felt the burden of responsibility to find the one correct path. I looked south, I looked north, and then I looked at my direction sheet for the fifth time, at least. This time, after the prayer, the spirit of God whispered to me, "You need to go farther."

We headed south, and we went farther than we had gone before, and, in about ten minutes, we found the exact path we were looking for; we found the right way, the only way down the canyon to the canyon floor. For over an hour, trying to proceed without the Lord's help, we were lost. With God's help, we immediately knew the correct direction to travel.

On that sacred day in Zion Park, a handful of young men and their leaders were reminded that God answers prayers and gives very specific directions to his children.

That feeling of being completely lost is a scary feeling. I am certain most of us have felt it on occasion. What if you went through your entire life being lost? Not knowing who you really are? Not really knowing why you exist? How would that feel? It would feel awful. It would be even worse if you were one phone call, one text, or one search away from knowing your exact location, your purpose and your potential destination. We can find our destination by going to the right source and searching as He has invited and commanded us to do.

A few years ago, an article in Time Magazine titled "Why Did Jesus Have to Die?" proposed a few theories from various theologians about Christ's death and shared the debates about His atonement. Some of "the thinkers" had a few correct ideas, but none of the responses were very thorough or completely accurate. ("Why Did Jesus Have to Die?" Time Magazine, April 12, 2004).

I invite you to please not get your spiritual information from Time Magazine. Despite proposing an inspiring question, the magazine should have referred readers to the right source for a correct answer to their profound question.

We access the source of all truth and receive specific answers from God by listening to a prophet of God, by reading from the word of God, and by praying to God and receiving manifestations, promptings and confirmation of the Spirit.

There are many who feel God would just let them know if they aren't going the right way. There are many who feel they don't have time to search. There are some who just don't care to search. There are others who simply have no desire to pursue the things of God.

An experience I had many years ago reminds me of the importance of taking the time to seek and embrace the truth.

I love Bosc pears. For those of you who haven't had a Bosc pear, they are delicious. I occasionally go grocery shopping, but not very often.

I had gone one week and bought a few fresh Bosc pears. When I got home, I ate one right away, and I intended to consume the rest of the pears over the next few days. I put one in my backpack, carefully positioning it in a little-used pocket for safekeeping, so I would have it for lunch at work the next day. The pear was going to be wonderful and delicious. Unfortunately, I completely forgot that I put it in the far recesses of my backpack. I never did remember to eat it that day and it didn't cross my mind for many days after that.

Life went on and I forgot the Bosc pear the next day and the next day and the next day. I forgot the pear for a long time. I finally remembered the pear, when, one day, after I noticed a terrible odor coming from my backpack, I searched for the source of the smell and, in that remote pocket, I found a now-compressed, dried pear (except the smell told me that it obviously wasn't dried properly). I had missed an opportunity for something delicious just because I forgot, I was too busy, and I just didn't pay attention.

We often act in a similar fashion when it comes to much more important facets of life. We fail to find the right way, the path to eternal life that Christ offers us, simply because we are busy with other things, we are inattentive or apathetic, so we overlook the truths and the details of godliness.

We fail to make this quest our biggest priority, so we miss sacred events and experiences, and never enjoy the real value of those things that are most wonderful and true.

It is a grave mistake for any of God's children to ignore God's designs. God has a perfect plan for each of us. His plan is a carefully crafted design; it was not made on a napkin over lunch. God has precise blueprints and diagrams for life. God wants to reveal the details and outlines, but will not unless we are interested in the specifics.

God wants to show us the eternal blueprints, to reveal to us our purposes, but He can only do so if we have a desire to be a part of building an eternal life with Him.

We must care enough about the order and the organization to discover the great and wonderful plan. Our goal then must be to find the way and to follow the path.

The Lord disagrees with those who frequently state; "It doesn't matter what faith you are, it doesn't matter what you believe, it's all the same anyway, as long as you just believe in God, as long as you are a good person; God will forgive everyone no matter what; Jesus died for everyone (He did, but there are some doctrines of accountability); God wouldn't be loving if He didn't save everyone."

If nothing really matters, if this anything-goes attitude is true, why would God have such exact instructions and detailed doctrines in the scriptures? Why is everything God does in perfect order? Why are the laws of physics absolute? Why is the earth in the only position that it could be in to sustain life?

Why would He have exact and concrete commandments, specific sermons and precise principles? Why would He have intricate instructions on how to perform ordinances?

I believe, as the scriptures state, that God is a God of perfection, He is a God of perfect order and that not one detail slips by Him.

His plan is precise and perfect, and He expects us to take the time to find Him and His truth through His doctrines, principles, promises, commandments and covenants.

Paul reminded us, *"For God is not the author of confusion, but of peace, as in all churches of the saints" (1 Corinthians 14:33).* The adversary is the creator of confusion, whose goal is to confuse, confound and corrupt the children of God; while a loving Father, the creator of clarity, invites us, with candor and simplicity, to experience the love, peace and salvation found in following His way. God is always all about the directives, details and direction.

Elder Dieter F. Uchtdorf shared this story of direction, degree and detail: "In 1979 a large passenger jet with 257 people on board left New Zealand for a sightseeing flight to Antarctica and back. Unknown to the pilots, however, someone had modified the flight coordinates by a mere two degrees. This error placed the aircraft 28 miles (45 km) to the east of where the pilots assumed, they were. As they approached Antarctica, the pilots descended to a lower altitude to give the passengers a better look at the landscape. Although both were experienced pilots, neither had made this particular flight before, and they had no way of knowing that the incorrect coordinates had placed them directly in the path of Mount Erebus, an active volcano that rises from the frozen landscape to a height of more than 12,000 feet (3,700 m).

As the pilots flew onward, the white of the snow and ice covering the volcano blended with the white of the clouds above, making it appear as though they were flying over flat ground. By the time the instruments sounded the warning that the ground was rising fast toward them, it was too late.

The airplane crashed into the side of the volcano, killing everyone on board" (Dieter F. Uchtdorf, "A Matter of a Few Degrees," April 2008 General Conference).

I believe God has broad arms, broad understanding, broad grace, and broad love, but a narrow set of principles, guidelines and commandments as He works according to perfect laws.

We must not rest until we get the answers, until we find and enter in the gate, until we live in the right way. I remember the story of a man, named Henry M. Leland, the founder of Cadillac, an automobile manufacturer, who would not rest until he made cars better.

This happened in the early 1900s, when cars were becoming popular and the demand was rising. The quality of the car was growing rapidly, with new innovations and improvements every year. One of the biggest problems with early automobiles was they were hard to start. Nearly every car at the time had to be hand cranked from the front. This took such strength that most women at the time weren't strong enough to rotate the hand crank that turned over the engine.

Even for most men, it was extremely difficult and dangerous to rotate the hand crank due to the resistance from the compression of the engines.

Henry M. Leland's mission was to change this. He wouldn't rest until he found the solution to make the automobile easier and safer to start. His deep determination started after his dear friend, Byron Carter, stopped to help a woman on the roadside to start her car one day. The man cranked her car and, in doing so, he broke his jaw when the engine resisted. The car started, and she was on her way, but the man was not okay.

The broken jaw got infected, and his dear friend soon died from complications and pneumonia.

This car manufacturer committed to focus his energy and efforts on coming up with a better way to start an automobile, so that people like his friend wouldn't die over starting a car. Within a few years of his commitment, he was able to design a better ignition system, all because of his focus on having specific questions and getting answers to those queries.

We must not rest until we get answers and gain a testimony of the truth. Then, we must not rest until we share these truths with those who are near and dear to us and to every honest in heart person seeking truth.

One Family Home Evening lesson I taught about searching for truth turned out to be one of the most insightful ever. During the lesson, we discussed how to go about asking, searching for, and, ultimately, receiving answers from God and the diligence required in this process of asking and receiving.

Our family owned a one-ounce gold coin worth about $1,200. Before the lesson, I took the coin outside in the backyard and buried it, covering it with about a half inch of dirt.

We began the lesson by discussing some verses of scripture. Then, I told my sons what I had done and said, "Whoever finds the gold, keeps it." All six of my boys immediately raced outside, intent on finding the coin. They wanted to be rich. They went out and searched and searched and searched—for less than ten minutes.

In my mind, it was a very weak search. They came back in the house, having been unsuccessful in their quest. Not one of them had really searched very hard. I told them I would leave the coin buried in the backyard for a week, so if they really wanted to search for it, they could find it and keep it.

A week went by and none of my children spent any time searching for the coin. I was somewhat puzzled, knowing my sons' love of money. On the other hand, it wasn't all that surprising, as I know that searching earnestly is a difficult process.

At the end of the week, I went and uncovered the coin and kept it for myself. The parable of the gold coin is a reminder to me that, as mortals, we are very resistant to making the effort to truly search. To search for truth, for understanding, for righteousness, for God, takes sustained effort, real intent, and sacrifice of time and of other worldly things.

There are many things my sons could have done that would have helped them in the search for the gold coin.

They could have invested some time, money and energy in finding a metal detector. They could have spent more than just a few minutes of cursory looking and, instead, could have carefully and methodically combed through the backyard. Certainly, a little more effort would have reaped a $1,200 reward. A little extra effort and exertion absolutely would have been worth the investment of energy and time.

God says His "elect" are those who *"hear my voice and harden not their hearts" (D&C 29:7)*. The elect seem to be those who have a desire and willingness to search. God loves a serious seeker of truth.

In high school, I worked at an ice arena. It was a great job and truly a lot of fun. I felt they put a lot of trust in us irresponsible sixteen- and seventeen-year-olds who pretty much ran the arena. One of my roles was to drive the Zamboni, which is the machine that cleans the ice and remakes new ice. I loved that part of the job.

One problem with operating the machine is that I really didn't know how it worked. I knew a few basic things, but didn't really understand how the Zamboni cut the ice and moved the shavings to the storage compartment and how the machine restored the new layers of ice. One day, the big Zamboni wasn't working like it should have. I wasn't certain why, but I felt it was getting bogged down with too much snow and ice. I decided to clear out the ice from the front area of the machine so it would work more effectively.

With the machine running, I reached over a trough and into where I felt the excess snow was. Suddenly and without warning, I heard a "zing" and felt intense pain.

I had reached into a big fan without even knowing it was there. Immediately, my last two fingers on my right hand were badly cut. I remember not wanting to even look, knowing the damage would be severe. It was a lesson I will never forget.

There is a serious risk to not knowing and not understanding and not researching and, instead, blindly reaching for information and direction. In life, the risk of not knowing where we came from, why we are here and where we are going is huge. We must know, we must take the time and make the effort to find out. Knowing critical truths and receiving critical answers brings peace and understanding as well as opportunity and clarity of vision.

The most important search any individual will ever conduct in their life is their search for God and his truth. Remember, God is a

God of order, He is not a God of confusion. He is our Father. He is our creator. He is our Redeemer. He is our light.

He is our salvation. He has invited us to follow Him and come unto Him. He has said, *"I am the way, the truth, and the life: no man cometh unto the Father, but by me" (John 14:6).*

So, what is the right way spiritually? My eleven-year-old son, Taft, came to me some time ago with the answer to that question.

We had been following the suggestions from Brother Devin Durrant's October 2015 General Conference talk to "ponderize" the scriptures as a family, meaning we were selecting a particular scripture to focus on, ponder and memorize each week. Taft came to me one day and said, *"Dad, I know our scripture for next week: 2 Nephi 25:29."*

In this verse Taft chose, Nephi tells us: *"And now behold, I say unto you that the right way is to believe in Christ, and deny him not; and Christ is the Holy One of Israel; wherefore ye must bow down before him, and worship him with all your might, mind, and strength, and your whole soul; and if ye do this ye shall in nowise be cast out" (2 Nephi 25:29).*

Nephi not only knew the right way, he traveled the right way and lived the right way.

Nephi's denotation of a right way implies that there are many other ways to travel in life, but only one correct way. After Nephi taught us the "right way," he summarized and solidified that a few verses later, saying: *"And now, behold, my beloved brethren, this is the way; and there is none other way nor name given under heaven whereby man can* be saved in the kingdom of God" (2 Nephi 31:21).

The Book of Mormon prophet, Alma, in some of his last words, wanted to impart important wisdom to his son, assuring him that; *"...there is no other way or means whereby man can be saved, only in and through Christ. Behold, he is the life the light of the world. Behold, he is the word of truth and righteousness"* (Alma 38:9).

For our dental offices in El Paso, Texas, we have a few cars that employees can drive as we have a handful of doctors who fly in to work from out of town. One of the cars is a Nissan Altima. It is a nice car, but it has one chronic, extremely annoying problem.

Every time someone gets in to drive the car and reaches to buckle the driver's-side seatbelt, the male portion of the metal buckle is not where it is supposed to be. The driver has to reach between the seat and the door to find the buckle, and, occasionally, even has to open the car door to locate the buckle.

I have driven cars for many years but, until we bought the Altima, I did not know about or appreciate something called a seatbelt button. The seatbelt button is fastened to the seatbelt to hold the buckle up high so that when you reach over your shoulder, the buckle is right there.

The Altima does not have a seatbelt button, and so the buckle slides down that side of the belt every time the seatbelt is released.

One of the other drivers of the Altima tried putting layers of tape under the buckle on the seatbelt to get the buckle to stay in its proper, elevated position. This has proven to be a less-than satisfactory solution.

The tape quickly wears out and falls off; or, even worse, it stays in place long enough that the sticky goo from the backing of the tape seeps out and gets all over the driver's clothes.

Now that I see its value, I have come to greatly appreciate even a simple seatbelt button. No car should go without one—ever.

I am aware this is a crude example, but I have learned that many principles and doctrines and truths are appreciated only when you don't have them, or when you have lost them or walked away from them.

Every principle matters. Every true principle is a blessing. When specific blessings are gone, there is a definite loss.

When my son, Tanner, was very young he collected Pokémon cards. He loved it, but he had an unusual approach to his collection. He would buy some cards, or his father would buy some for him, and then he would put his favorite ones in a plastic cover sheet in a binder. Cards he didn't like wouldn't go into the binder.

As his father, I coached him on the importance of collecting complete sets of things, but he wasn't buying into the complete set approach and was definitive about the cards he liked and the ones he didn't like.

He took this to the extreme, hiding cards he didn't like and, on a few occasions even attempting to flush precious cards down the toilet. I would take them from him to preserve them and then, later, when he wasn't paying attention, I would put them into his binder.

Within a day or two, he would comb through his binder, recognize cards he didn't like and, try again to bid good riddance to those cards by hiding or flushing them away.

It was hard to teach Tanner, but I was trying to show him that there was great value in having the complete collection. I wanted him to know that the greatest value was in the entire set, rather than just a piece of the set. In time, he seemed to learn this.

We are the same way with truth, we often embrace slices of truth and sections of the scriptures, and portions of the gospel, but we reject other critical pieces that may be more uncomfortable for us or harder to live.

God's right way is also His complete way. God does not work in half-truths or partial truths or deceptive doctrines; He doesn't lead you down just a section of the straight and narrow path. God is perfect, He is complete, He is thorough, He will show us the entire path and the entire truth. We would be amiss if we walked the path far enough to get close to God's neighborhood, but didn't have the final address to get us into His kingdom.

The gospel of Jesus Christ is like a great puzzle of life. As you come to know it is the Savior's puzzle, you will begin to put the pieces together as He shows you how they fit. As the pieces (principles) come together, the picture is more and more clear. The gospel of Jesus Christ has all the puzzle pieces necessary to see clearly what you are building and for entrance into the kingdom of God. You will never be able to see the complete picture of the kingdom of God while walking a wrong path with so many pieces to the puzzle missing. He will lovingly show us the pieces to the puzzle: one piece or a few pieces at a time if we will ask Him and participate in assembling the puzzle.

I recently watched a video of a dog. This was not a normal dog. This dog had been raised with rabbits. He had been surrounded by rabbits and exposed to their ways his entire life. He did not know the way of a dog.

The video shows the dog chasing around the backyard but, instead of running like a normal dog, this dog is hopping, back and forth, all across the backyard. This hopping is what he observed and then emulated.

In many ways, this dog had become like a rabbit. He was following the rabbit way, not the way of the dog.

As was obvious from the video, the dog was not able to run as fast as he should or could have. Acting like a rabbit, and not a dog interfered with his ability and inhibited his full potential.

I have witnessed many individuals attempt to do things "the way others are doing it" or "the recommended way" or "the way of the world" or even "their own way."

There are hundreds of alternatives to the right way; yet, any other way than the right way is always less effective, less appropriate, less helpful, and less successful in getting us to a secure destination with God. Any other way that is not God's way is the wrong way.

There will always be alternatives to the right way. We need to be able to recognize those alternatives for what they are.

God's truths are not found in one principle or one doctrine, rather an intricate set of principles and doctrines that are all true. Elder Carlos E. Asay reminded us, "... *we succeed because we are teaching the fulness of the gospel of Jesus Christ as restored in this day. We don't play, as Elder Packer has taught, on one key; we play the entire keyboard" (Asay, Carlos E., "A Missionary Opportunity," April 3, 1976).*

The keyboard is a great reminder of the beauty of the sound of all the principles of the gospel of Jesus Christ woven together in perfect pitch and perfect harmony.

Yet, as mentioned earlier—this perfect harmony—or at least putting ourselves in perfect harmony with God—does not always come easy.

Every person who travels the right way knows, there are no shortcuts to the kingdom of God, no imitations that suffice to get us to the celestial kingdom. Many people in life will resist doing hard things, they won't accept uncomfortable assignments, or commit to increased obedience to push themselves a litter further.

We often resist growth, because this is not the way we want growth to come. We want growth to come easily. Yet, "our ways" or our methods, are not God's ways or God's methods. God's pathway is a trail of growth and progress, filled with obstacles, adversity, challenges, and opportunities. Interestingly, we are also the recipients of special, unique kinds of help along the way—which we also fail to recognize if we are content to travel the wrong way. God's plan is motivated and inspired by our potential to become like our Heavenly Father. After all, He is our Father, and *"we are the offspring of God" (Acts 17: 29).*

When I was in dental school, we were taught how to cast metal using the lost wax technique. You can create anything in metal— any ring, trinket, locket, charm, bracelet, or anything else made of precious metal—using this technique.

When you have created what you want in wax, you place the wax into an investment material, which is like a cement. When the investment hardens, you then heat up the investment to burn out the wax, leaving a pattern of what you are designing in the investment material.

You then put your gold or metal into a crucible that can be heated. The crucible is placed in a centrifuge. As the metal heats, it liquifies and the impurities are burned off. When the metal is in its liquid state and purified, it is thrown by the centrifuge into the investment material and it immediately hardens where the wax used to be. The metal is now in the shape of the old wax mold.

When the metal cools, you break off the investment material and find a rough-looking product that is dull and a little crude.

A series of stones are used to burnish, shape and smooth the metal. Next, polishes and pumices are used to further burnish the gold, until it is shiny and shimmering. In the end, the metal looks beautiful, it looks golden.

This is the same technique our Heavenly Father uses with us. God has a pattern and a process. He allows us to be put in a crucible of heat, trial and affliction. Life's crucibles of affliction are not always the means we want or hope for, but those trials are necessary to purify us. Along with the crucible of affliction, He also continues to shape, refine, smooth, burnish and polish us, even when we think He should be done. This is all part of the development of gifts, traits, character and God-like attributes. In the end, we are truly golden if we are humble enough to allow Him to refine our lives. The process truly is remarkable to watch and, when you understand it, it is a beautiful process to be a part of. It is wonderful to have a Father that desires us to be golden like Himself through a very exacting process.

I have heard many who have been invited to follow Jesus Christ say things like: 'I want to be my own person,' 'I want to be unique,' I want to be different,' 'I don't want to be like everyone else,' 'I don't want to change who I am,' 'I still want to be a fun person,' 'I don't want to become a robot,' 'I don't want to seem too spiritual,' 'I want to be free and without restrictions,' 'I don't want to be just like every other follower of Christ.'

These comments and the attitudes behind them are based on excuses, deception and on a lack of understanding of the "right way" and of what we can truly become.

Think of the deficiencies in this argument. Christ has asked us to follow Him and to be like Him. Could there be anything better that we could be or become through our lives than to become the personification of Christ, with the perfect attributes of Christ? No! Of course, this takes sacrifice and effort, and giving up the world. Is it worth it? Of course.

Remember the goals of the adversary are, as Nephi stated: *"... that they might pervert the right ways of the Lord, that they might blind the eyes and harden the hearts of the children of men" (1 Nephi 13:27).*

The right way truly is to "believe in Christ and deny him not." The right way is to follow Christ and strive to become like Him. The right way is to discover exactly what Christ would have you do and be.

The right way is God's precise way, God's planned way, with God's specific, outlined directives, not an alternative way, or an abbreviated way, or a way developed through the ideas of supposed wise men with supposed wise interpretations of scripture.

Elder Peterson put it this way: "There are some who don't understand that there is no right way to do something wrong" (H. Burke Peterson, "As a Beacon on a Hill," Ensign, Nov. 1974, pg. 68).

No matter what man may say, God is still the only author of all truth, and He has promised:

"Ask, and it shall be given you; seek, and ye shall find; knock, and it shall be opened unto you" (Matthew 7:7).

"[A]nd if ye shall ask with a sincere heart, with real intent, having faith in Christ, he will manifest the truth of it unto you," Moroni taught us (Moroni 10:4).

And, Alma said, in his great discourse on faith: *"But behold, if ye will awake and arouse your faculties, even to an experiment upon my words, and exercise a particle of faith, yea, even if ye can no more than desire to believe, let this desire work in you, even until ye believe in a manner that ye can give place for a portion of my words" (Alma 32:27).*

All of these words and verses are merely invitations to find Him and His truth. This should be the primary purpose of our existence, and it is the one quest in life that makes every other quest pale in comparison. I love to call this the Particle Principle. If you give God a particle of desire, He will greatly reward even that small effort. Of course, this doesn't mean that you can sit back and wait for Him to do all the work.

I remember when my daughter, Holland, turned six. That morning we were doing some chores around the house, while she was still in bed. Suddenly, in the middle of this morning ritual, I got a call from her room on our home intercom system. I picked up and she said, "Dad, are you bringing me breakfast in bed?" She had some high expectations.

I hope we don't have the same expectations of God. I hope we don't sit back and wait for breakfast in bed. I hope we aren't caught *"standing idle in the marketplace" too long. (See Matthew 20:3.)* I hope we "go and search until" we find. This requires us to search, pray and study with "real intent."

` Christ shared two brief metaphors that illustrate what I am trying to say.

First, He says, *"Again, the kingdom of heaven is like unto treasure hid in a field; the which when a man hath found, he hideth, and for joy thereof goeth and selleth all that he hath, and buyeth that field."*

Second, He adds,

"Again, the kingdom of heaven is like unto a merchant man, seeking goodly pearls:

"Who, when he had found one pearl of great price, went and sold all that he had, and bought it" (Matthew 13:44-46).

The question for each of us is: "Are we willing to give up everything for the truth, for the right way, for the right direction back to God?" God has every answer we need if we are willing to ask and respond to his invitation.

Randall K. Bennett, of the Seventy, taught: "In reality we have only two eternal choices, each with eternal consequences: choose to follow the Savior of the world and thus choose eternal life with our Heavenly Father or choose to follow the world and thus choose to separate ourselves from Heavenly Father eternally.

We cannot successfully choose both the safety of righteousness and the dangers of worldliness" (Randall K. Bennett, "Choose

Eternal Life," October 2011 General Conference).

The Holy Ghost Will Show Us

Sally, a wonderful manager for our company, is also a dear friend of mine. A few years ago, I had a very specific impression to invite her to a fireside. She accepted the invitation, came to the fireside, and even brought her son. During the meeting, she felt the Holy Ghost distinctly tell her that what was happening was good. At the time, she was a member of a different faith.

As we spoke after the meeting, Sally said, "I am really feeling something here."

I explained that she was feeling the Spirit and that the Spirit was teaching her and testifying to her of truth. She recognized God was leading her in the right direction.

Over the next few weeks, she took the missionary lessons and prayed and knew she should be baptized. It was a simple process for her, once she felt the Spirit of God leading and directing her to the correct path.

Sally now steadily walks down that path, partaking of the fruit of the tree of life, savoring every minute of it and sharing it with others. Sally found the golden coin because she was willing to make the effort of acting on promptings she had received.

In our search for truth, we must never forget these precious words from the Apostle Paul 2000 years ago who said:

"Eye hath not seen, nor ear heard, neither have entered into the heart of man,

the things which God hath prepared for them that love him.

But God hath revealed them unto us by his Spirit: for the Spirit searcheth all things, yea, the deep things of God.

For what man knoweth the things of a man, save the spirit of man which is in him? even so the things of God knoweth no man, but the Spirit of God.

Now we have received, not the spirit of the world, but the spirit which is of God; that we might know the things that are freely given to us of God.

Which things also we speak, not in the words which man's wisdom teacheth, but which the Holy Ghost teacheth; comparing spiritual things with spiritual.

But the natural man receiveth not the things of the Spirit of God: for they are foolishness unto him: neither can he know them, because they are spiritually discerned" *(1 Corinthians 2:9-14).*

The message I would like you to remember from these verses is that we can only know the things of God through the Spirit of God. To find the right way, we must seek and search for the Spirit of God to teach us His truths.

As we do so, these six tips will help with our discovery:

First: Trust the feeling of the Spirit; it will be more powerful than perceived facts. We can only understand God's principles through the Spirit of God.

Second: Apply the truths to know of their truthfulness.

Third: Pray to know.

Fourth: Search the scriptures; the word of God will tell you what to do.

Fifth: Repeat. Remember, truth will be enlightening and delicious. It will feel good, and you will want to keep feeding your soul with more of this wonderful feeling.

Sixth: Expect the promise *"he that diligently seeketh shall find" to happen for you (1 Nephi 10:19)*. This is not just a statement, but a promise from a loving Father to His children.

Remember, in our discovery, it is His path, His safe and peaceful path, we are seeking. In Proverbs, we read: *"In all thy ways acknowledge him, and he shall direct thy paths" (Proverbs 3:6)*.

The Psalmist wrote: *"Thy word is a lamp unto my feet, and a light unto my path." (Psalms 119:105)* and Nephi refers to the word of God as an iron rod and teaches that, *"by clinging to the word of God, we will be able to safely walk the path, withstanding temptation, never losing our way, never perishing." (See 1 Nephi 15:23-24).*

A few years ago, Brad, a friend of mine, sat down to listen to the missionaries. He was curious, but not really interested. He was dating a young lady who was a member of the Church of Jesus Christ of Latter-day saints. He felt that the Church was an okay thing but not really for him. Before the first missionary lesson, he said, "I will listen, but will not get baptized."

I respected his feelings, and I didn't really expect much to come out of our meeting.

Yet, it was amazing to see his change of heart during the course of the first lesson. As the missionaries taught him, the Spirit of God (spirit of truth) entered the room.

The Holy Ghost, in no uncertain terms, taught Brad that what he was hearing was truth and the right way.

As the spirit of the meeting increased, one of the missionaries asked Brad if he would be baptized. I was shocked to hear Brad say yes. Just thirty minutes earlier he had made it clear that he was going to listen only out of curiosity, but he had no desire to be baptized.

Yet, the Spirit, in less than an hour, had enlightened and redirected Brad, and had pointed him in a different direction. The Spirit now had him traveling the right way.

Similar to taking a test and knowing the answers, being on the right pathway brings a sense of confidence and peace. I remember, as a young missionary, being filled with confidence as we went about the work, and all because we knew we had all the necessary answers that people needed to build faith in Christ.

I remember being asked questions like, 'Why do accidents and other bad things happen?', 'Why do kids die young?', 'Why is there war?', 'Why are we here on earth?', 'Why is Christ so important?', 'Is there really a plan?', 'Does God really exist?', 'How can God love everyone?', 'How can I feel the love of God?', 'What about people who never heard of Christ?', 'Where are my loved ones who have died?', 'What about handicapped people, are they being punished in some way?' and 'Why do so many people have to suffer?'

I was asked each of these questions by people who truly desired answers that satisfied. Then, as now, I enjoyed fielding any and all questions because truth is reassuring, satisfying and wonderful.

I know that Heavenly Father hasn't given every single answer yet, but He has given every answer necessary to increase faith and allow us to go forward in faith.

The plethora of answers we do have allows us to strengthen our faith and helps us "to know," one principle at a time.

The Lord said of the righteous, *"And to them will I reveal all mysteries, yea, all the hidden mysteries of my kingdom from days of old, and for ages to come, will I make known unto them the good pleasure of my will concerning all things pertaining to my kingdom" (D&C 76: 7).*

I love this example of an approach to finding the truth: Elder David E. Sorensen spoke of a man who worked for the United States Treasury Department as a counterfeit expert.

This man had just broken up a major counterfeit ring and was fielding questions at a press conference.

"One of the reporters directed this statement to him: 'You must spend a lot of time studying counterfeit bills to recognize them so easily.'" I love his reply, as it is applicable to all those who understand God and His ways.

'No, I don't ever study counterfeit bills, I spend my time studying genuine bills; then the imperfection is easy to recognize.'" (David E. Sorensen, "The Blessing of Work," CES Fireside for Young Adults, March 6, 2005, Brigham Young University).

Shouldn't we be doing the same when it comes to studying the scriptures, and the gospel and finding the right way God has revealed? Shouldn't we be so engaged in studying and living principles that bring edification and light and truth, that we have no time for the counterfeit doctrines of the world?

Only true principles—learned and applied—bring lasting peace and happiness. The Book of Mormon prophets teach us much about the rewards of seeking after true principles. True principles, as Alma taught, enlighten our minds, enlarge our hearts and become delicious to us.

Mormon reminded us that true principles come from God, and *"...behold, that which is of God inviteth and enticeth to do good continually; wherefore, everything which inviteth and enticeth to do good, and to love God, and to serve him, is inspired of God"* *(Moroni 7:13).*

In this dispensation, too, the Lord has taught us that truth edifies us. *"And that which doth not edify is not of God, and is darkness" (D&C 50:23).*

I have been reminded time and time again of the importance of entering "in by the way"—and of staying there. Indeed, Nephi teaches this powerful doctrine, saying: *"For behold, again I say unto you that if ye will enter in by the way, and receive the Holy Ghost, it will show unto you all things what ye should do" (2 Nephi 32:5).*

I have learned, as Nephi declares, that the Holy Ghost will show us truth, will show us the way, and, in the end, will show us the true facts about God. I have observed in my life how powerful these feelings from God, through the Holy Ghost, can be. I have observed that we can trust impressions, promptings, observations and insights over what "experts" or authorities might state is a fact.

I will never forget, as a fourteen-year-old, receiving a patriarchal blessing promising me that one day I would be a bishop. I felt that everything in that blessing was true and would happen one day. The reality of the situation was that if you had inquired of the other 400 people in my ward at the time, I am certain they would have said that there was no way in this lifetime that Jeff Erickson would be a bishop. Yet, I knew; and I knew that God knew.

God gives us feelings to reveal truth. This truth about me being a bishop came thirty years after the patriarch's impression and prompting.

President George Albert Smith shared this about the power of spiritual feelings: "A Holland brother by the name of Folkers was living with his wife at my place, and they could not speak or understand the English language. He used to go to the fast meetings [Sunday church meetings], and when the other people talked, he could not understand what they said. When they finished, he would get up and talk, and we could not understand him. One day I asked him, 'Why do you go to the English-speaking services? You cannot understand.' It took me some time to make him understand what I wanted to know. Finally, he smiled and said: 'It is not what you hear that makes you happy; not what you see that makes you happy; it is what you feel, and I can feel just as well as anybody'" (George Albert Smith, Conference Report, October 1947, pg. 2-8).

To find truth, we must allow the Holy Ghost to be able to touch our hearts, minds and spirit and to feel the truth. I understand what Brother Folkers meant. I have sat through many home coming talks by returning missionaries.

Often, these missionaries close with a testimony in a different language, the language of their mission. I have heard testimonies in Spanish, Japanese or Portuguese and have had no idea what was being said. Despite not knowing what I am hearing, I have been able to feel powerfully the truth of their words. Several times, during these sacred and heartfelt testimonies of truth, I have been overwhelmed by spiritual feelings.

The Lord will give you answers to your heartfelt questions in life. Truth fears no trial. Truth conquers all things. Truth prevails when all else fails. Truth is of God. Truth is available from God. Truth is the basis for God's wonderful plan. Truth is what we need in order to live after the manner of happiness

As we ask the Lord for answers, for truth, for guidance, the Spirit will come and tell us, show us, instruct us, or reveal to us the way.

Try Alma's taste test. I believe it is a powerful way to assist us in making decisions. Alma taught:

"Now, we will compare the word unto a seed. Now, if ye give place, that a seed may be planted in your heart, behold, if it be a true seed, or a good seed, if ye do not cast it out by your unbelief, that ye will resist the Spirit of the Lord, behold, it will begin to swell within your breasts; and when you feel these swelling motions, ye will begin to say within yourselves—It must needs be that this is a good seed, or that the word is good, for it beginneth to enlarge my soul; yea, it beginneth to enlighten my understanding, yea, it beginneth to be delicious to me" (Alma 32:28).

When we make decisions, we must ponder and pray and, then, we should weigh our decisions against five simple factors, asking ourselves:

1. "Is it something that is good?"

2. "Does it enlarge my soul?"

3. "Does it enlighten my mind?"

4. "Is it delicious to me?"

And, finally,

5. "Does it feel good and right inside?"

This may seem oversimplified, but, without question, every bad decision I have made has not felt right from the beginning. With those bad decisions, I have usually known in my mind or in my heart, that the thing I was about to say or do was not the right thing. With really bad decisions, the feelings were even more profound, distinct and obvious. This is absolutely in line with the doctrine taught by Mormon:

"For behold, my brethren, it is given unto you to judge, that ye may know good from evil; and the way to judge is as plain, that ye may know with a perfect knowledge, as the daylight is from the dark night.

For behold, the Spirit of Christ is given to every man, that he may know good from evil; wherefore, I show unto you the way to judge; for everything which inviteth to do good, and to persuade to believe in Christ, is sent forth by the power and gift of Christ; wherefore ye may know with a perfect knowledge it is of God.

But whatsoever thing persuadeth men to do evil, and believe not in Christ, and deny him, and serve not God, then ye may know with a perfect knowledge it is of the devil; for after this manner doth the devil work, for he persuadeth no man to do good, no, not one; neither do his angels; neither do they who subject themselves unto him" (Moroni 7:15-17).

The Lord has taught us in many ways how to judge. We must choose to judge or decide righteously.

Nephi taught, *"For behold, thus saith the Lord God: I will give unto the children of men line upon line, precept upon precept, here a little and there a little; and blessed are those who hearken unto my precepts, and lend an ear unto my counsel, for they shall learn wisdom; for unto him that receiveth I will give more; and from them that shall say, We have enough, from them shall be taken away even that which they have" (2 Nephi 28: 30).*

One summer, many years ago, when I was serving as a full-time missionary, my companion and I were teaching the White family. They enjoyed the message and enjoyed listening to us, but they didn't seem to know if what we were teaching was true. One evening, we had a very powerful discussion. The spirit was present, and it was testifying to them, telling them that what we were teaching was from God and was true.

At one point during that spirit-filled discussion, we extended an invitation to follow Christ, inviting them to follow their hearts and their feelings and act in accordance with the will of God.

We invited Robert, the father, to be baptized and he agreed. He was recognizing the voice of God, and choosing the right way. We then extended the invitation to the mother, Carolyn. She said she wasn't ready for baptism. We told her we respected her desires. We then turned to their oldest son, Jason, who was about fourteen at the time, and asked, "Will you be baptized?" He said,

"Yes." He was feeling the spirit of God testify to him.

His mother was surprised and she turned and asked him, "Jason, why do you want to be baptized?"

Jason, who was a baseball player, said to her, "Mom, you know how it feels to win the championship game?"

"Yes," she responded.

"Well, Mom, I feel that right now and so I want to be baptized."

Here was a powerful lesson from a fourteen-year-old who was feeling the presence of God and the spirit of God directing him to take a step forward. He was willing to act because God was telling him to act through sacred feelings.

Jeffrey Erickson

When Jason's mother heard his words, she suddenly opened her heart to the spirt and said, "I, too, want to be baptized." The spirit of God was in that room directing, guiding, and inviting people to follow the path, to go the right way. This good family responded by saying, "I am willing to follow God."

Jason, at fourteen, and his parents learned something they hadn't really known before.

"But when the Comforter is come, whom I will send unto you from the Father, even the Spirit of truth, which proceeded from the Father, he shall testify of me" (John 15:26).

Jason knew that day that God had touched him through the spirit. I love that the Holy Ghost or spirit of God is called the spirit of truth.

The mission of the Holy Ghost is to testify of the truths of Jesus Christ. When the Holy Ghost testifies to us, we feel it and then we know. Why? Because it is truth being taught and received.

Sometimes, when we know a little, we assume we know a lot. This is a particularly dangerous approach when it comes to our relationship with Jesus Christ. It is not enough just to know of Jesus Christ, we must come to know the truth about Him and His principles. We must seek as much knowledge about Him as we can. We must "find Him" through prayer, information, scriptural study, testing His principles, and application of His truths. In this way, we come to know Him more personally.

There was a time when my four-year-old son, Tyler, thought his knowledge of spelling was perfect. He thought he knew enough about spelling to spell a variety of words. He knew a few words, but his knowledge was far from complete.

One Saturday night, my family and I were eating dinner. My wife said to me, "We need to give Tanner [our two-year-old son], some M-I-L-K," and she spelled it out so Tanner wouldn't know what it was. Tyler, his brother, was learning to spell and, for some reason, he knew how to spell milk perfectly. He said, "Yeah, Tanner needs some milk." I could see a look of pride on his face about his spelling knowledge. He then chimed up and boldly said, "And, I would like some N-A-D-O apple juice." He had knowledge about spelling, but it was pretty incomplete. Sometimes we think we know all the truth, when, in actuality, we still have so much to learn. Are we ever learning and, yet, never coming to a knowledge of the truth? I hope we are not.

Like Tyler's knowledge, our knowing one small piece of truth is not enough. We need to continue to search and to discover the many treasures and truths of the gospel of Jesus Christ. We also need to be focused and committed to doing what we know and feel is right as we pursue God's truth.

Cheetahs have a few powerful features that help them to survive and keep them focused on their prey. They have "tear marks" that run from the inside corners of their eyes down to the outside edges of their mouth.

These marks help them to focus. The dark marks actually reflect the glare of the sun when they are hunting during the day. The marks also act like the sights on a rifle. While they are running, the marks help to keep the cheetah aiming at its prey while it chases for the hunt.

A constant focus on truth, a focus on righteousness, a focus on searching, a focus on powerful decisions, a commitment to truth will help us to aim at celestial and eternal rewards without being deceived by telestial traps.

One other principle in finding truth is direct application. The Savior taught the Jews a powerful principle in the temple: Jesus answered them, and said, "My doctrine is not mine, but His that sent me."

If any man will do his will, he shall know of the doctrine, whether it be of God, or whether I speak of myself" (John 7:16-17). Living a commandment, a principle, a truth, or a doctrine will reveal the truth of the information to us. Nephi said of God that, "*he proveth all his words" (2 Nephi 11:3).*

I have a sister who is not a member of the Church of Jesus Christ of Latter-day Saints, but she lived the principle of tithing for many years. Why would she give up ten percent of her money when she was not even committed to the Church? Because, she was committed to the truthfulness of the principle of the tithe. She knew it was true because she had lived it and it worked. She knew the principle came from God and not from man.

Dangers In Not Finding The Way

There are absolute "privileges of the path" that come when you walk the right way. These privileges include peace, power, perfect principles, knowledge, faith in Christ, assurance, and the most important being the opportunity to enter *"the gate of heaven" (Helaman 3:28)*. We sometimes forget "the narrowness of the gate." We also tend to forget "the keeper of the gate," that the "gate is strait," and that the purpose of the gate is "repentance and baptism by water."

Jacob said, *"O then, my beloved brethren, come unto the Lord, the Holy One. Remember that his paths are righteous. Behold, the way for man is narrow, but it lieth in a straight course before him, and the keeper of the gate is the Holy One of Israel; and he employeth no servant there; and there is none other way save it be by the gate; for he cannot be deceived, for the Lord God is his name"* (2 Nephi 9:41).

The gate of Christ is the only way, it is the right way. We can find our destination by going to the right source and searching as He has invited and commanded us to do

Many years ago, I heard of a man who got baptized into the Church when he was 91 years old. I had two thoughts. First, that his experience was both happy and sad. How difficult to not know the right way for 91 years. The second and more powerful thought was how comforting and invigorating it must have been to finally find the right path after 91 years of not knowing where the pathway to happiness was.

A few years ago, I met a wonderful woman named Ginger, who was in in her late thirties. She had just been introduced to the gospel of Jesus Christ through a friend.

She loved the newly discovered doctrines, principles, covenants and commandments. She was amazed at these truths.

I will never forget an interview I had with her as her future bishop. She was preparing for her baptism, and we had a powerful discussion. She said something unforgettable. She said, "My only regret is that no one told me sooner."

Yes, 30+ years is late, but so much better than 40 or 50. I am grateful for people who come to know how wonderful the kingdom of God is here on the earth. It is always better to come late than to never arrive. There is danger in never knowing.

There is also danger—so much more danger—in discovering the path, in being on the path, and then diverting from it.

Elder Marvin J. Ashton shared this story in General Conference years ago: He said, "I recall a twelve-year-old boy standing in front of a large congregation to share his testimony. As he stood trembling in fear and emotion, his voice failed him. He stood speechless; our hearts went out to him.

The creeping seconds dragged on, making the silence of the moment intense. Prayerfully we hoped that he might gain composure and the ability to express his

95

testimony. After great uneasiness and anxiety peculiar to a young person in such a circumstance, he raised his bowed head and softly said, 'Brothers and sisters, my testimony is too small.' He cleared his voice and sat down" (Marvin J. Ashton, "The Power of Plainness," April 1977 General Conference).

Many individuals are in the same predicament as the young man Elder Ashton talked about and do not have a testimony of these principles yet! If you are one off those individuals, that is okay and appropriate. You—and all the rest of us—just never give up. We must take the time to grow the testimony. We must continue to press forward with a steadfastness in Christ. As Alma said, testimonies start as a seed and grow with appropriate nourishment.

Peter taught about those who have discovered the truth, but departed from it.

He referenced, *"...which have forsaken the right way, and are gone astray," (2 Peter 2:15)*. This seems to be a growing group. As the perceived wisdom of the world fictitiously grows the, perception is that God's voice, influence, power and wisdom is no longer needed.

I had a conversation with a dear friend who had been struggling with his testimony. This somehow became an excuse for him to excuse the commandments in his life. Suddenly, he found himself committing serious sin.

His life was a mess, and you could readily see that in his countenance. He blamed his darkened state on not being sure if the Church was true. Despite wondering about his testimony, he stated to me, "I was sure a lot happier when I was living the principles." This is always true, because the principles are true and living principles.

I have seen people lose faith, lose family, lose opportunity, lose trust, lose precious relationships; in fact, I have seen people quit the path and, in so doing, lose everything of true value on this earth and eternal blessings as well.

I will never forget having to make a tough decision as a bishop one day. There was a young man desiring baptism and he wanted his father to perform the ordinance. The father wanted to perform the ordinance also even though he wasn't right with God. I remember pleading for help in deciding what to do. The Lord gave me a very specific answer to my query. The spirit told me that the father was not qualified for the honor and blessing of performing the ordinance at this time. It was a tough pill for that father, a missed opportunity for someone who was not doing what he could to walk the right way.

Moroni reminded us that when our faith dwindles, the Lord's hand is limited in our lives. *"And the reason why he ceaseth to do miracles among the children of men is because that they dwindle in unbelief, and depart from the right way, and know not the God in whom they should trust"* *(Mormon 9:20).*

Blessings of Finding the Right Way

Here is a potent promise to the obedient: *"He that keepeth his commandments receiveth truth and light, until he is glorified in truth and knoweth all things" (D&C 93:28).*

I have learned that when we find out the truth about God, we find out the truth about ourselves. We realize who we are and who we can become. We are children of God, and we can become like Him, living forever with Him.

A fascinating story came of out Iceland a few years ago. On a sightseeing adventure a busload of tourists stopped to see some beautiful volcanic beds. After they reloaded the bus, a few passengers noticed that a certain lady, a member of the tour, was missing.

The other passengers alerted the driver to the fact that one of the tour members was missing. The passengers got off the bus again and began an extensive search for the missing tourist. This all started in the evening. Every member of the tour searched and searched the area for the lady. They were having no success, but they continued searching until nearly 3:00 a.m.

About this time, one of the searchers, an elderly lady, began to realize that the description of the missing lady sounded like her. It was then that she reported herself found. She had changed her clothes before she had gotten back on the bus, and she had looked different to her fellow tourists.

In our search for answers, for truth, for the spirit, for meaning, for God, may we find ourselves. I love that when we do find God and follow him, we are changed and, in many instances, our behaviors, attitudes and actions are no longer recognizable, and we find out who we can become.

I served as a bishop during the recession of 2006 to 2012. Elder Claudio R. M. Costa, of the Presidency of the Seventy, visited our stake to preside over stake conference. He held several meetings, one of them with all the bishops in the stake to provide counsel and direction. As bishops, we were able to ask him some direct questions.

It was a great meeting, and I recall that the direction he provided was wonderful, but out of all the things he said, there is really only one piece of counsel that I remember distinctly from that day without referring to notes.

Elder Costa gave this memorable counsel in response to a question that was asked. The question was, "Elder Costa, what do we tell the people in our wards who are losing homes and jobs and who are struggling so badly financially?" His answer made a powerful impression upon me. He simply said, "Teach them the principles!"

I remember looking for a different answer, a more powerful answer—potentially a jobs program, a list of five steps to economic recovery, a bailout program or some other fancy sounding initiative. In reality, he brought the answer and program that is most powerful of all. He brought God's way and God's program. It was a simple and straightforward answer and, yet, it hit me with immense power! He reminded me that God's ways are higher than mens'.

A "high way" can mean a more elevated approach to life. An elevated vantage point is a place where it is easier to see the wisdom of God and where you see things in a more heavenly light.

A "high way" of God lets you see things from a Godly perspective, so you see more than you ever could imagine seeing. You see more majesty and more mercy—all with a clarity and beauty that only heights can bring.

A "high way" is a greater way. It is the best way to look at life. You see life full of faith, hope and charity. You see the opportunity in every trial and challenge. You see the hand of God in every experience.

A "high way" will always be different from a way of the world. A "high way" will always be the road less traveled. The "high way" path is a lonely path, but the scenery and serenity there far outweigh the mire and crowded streets of lower paths.

A "high way" is a lighted way. It is not a path of darkness or sin. In is not a path of gray. It is a well-lit, well-marked, well-paved, and well-kept path. It is a path that truly is lit by the light of Christ. The path is perfect, precise, and protected.

Finally, the "high ways" of God are simply more pure. They are ways that bring no remorse. They are paths that bring no regret. They are paths that bless and inspire. The "high ways" of God are the real pathways of true prosperity. The "high ways" of God bring holiness, peace, contentment, and spiritual satisfaction. The "high ways" of

God are the ways of eternal and never-ending happiness.

I testify that there is greater power in the principles of God than in anything the world has to offer, because the principles of God are absolutely true and come from a loving and omniscient Father and a loving and sacrificing Son. These principles have the answers to life's most important queries and the solutions to life's biggest challenges.

There is something earth-shattering, something life-altering, something exciting, something mentally enlightening, and something absolutely wonderful about discovering who God is, who Jesus Christ is, why the atonement is the centerpiece of life, what God's plan is, where we came from, why we came to earth, where we go when we leave here, and every wonderful principle and doctrine that make so much sense and give us so much peace.

Jeffrey Erickson

The Power in Finding the Right Way

There is power in discovering the right way. A few years ago, a powerful discovery was made in the area of art. There was a painting that had sat in an attic for nearly 100 years. The owners felt it was of little worth. It changed hands and then, in 1991, someone noticed that it had familiar tones to a Van Gogh, and so they had it evaluated. Unfortunately, at that time it was deemed not to be a Van Gogh. However, the owners continued to feel that it was real, so, after 22 more years they sought to have it evaluated again.

Changes in evaluation methods had taken place, and a critical letter from Van Gogh himself had been discovered. This time, in 2013, when it was evaluated by the experts, they deemed it an authentic Van Gogh. It was valued at $50 million. The painting is called "Sunset at Montmajour." Like this painting, finding the right way helps us to discover who we really are and our true value in the eyes of God. Discovery can take time, expertise, experience and spiritual testing. In the end, discovery will always be worth the time it takes.

What are the blessings of doing things the "right way?" There are many. First, when you travel the right way you arrive at the right destination. There is frustration, sorrow and sadness for those who have no idea where they are really heading. Second, when you travel the right way, you travel with more peace. You can actually enjoy the journey because you understand why the journey is hard. Third, when you travel the right way, you are guided by a God who desires to help you reach your destination. Fourth, when you go your "own way" you can never reach God's eternal destination. Certainly, there is power in traveling the "right way."

Years ago, on his way to a father and sons outing in the Pinal Mountains of Arizona, one of the ward members, a friend of mine, had missed a sign, made a wrong turn and had gone the wrong way—the long way— around the mountain. He kept going, thinking that, somehow, the wrong turn would be resolved easily a few miles down the road. What should have been a rather simple, two-hour trip became a five-hour, unnerving sojourn. When he finally reached the campsite, he was tired, beyond frustrated and not in good spirits.

For him, taking the wrong turn had ruined a potentially wonderful trip.

I have seen frustrated and sad people in life who have taken the wrong turn. They have followed a foolish path, or they have missed some wonderful opportunities.

When you travel the "right way," you know that Christ is on your side, and that Christ is traveling with you. Paul said, *"If God be for us, who can prevail against us" (Romans 8:31 JST).*

Believing in Christ means trusting in His ways. Believing in Christ means trusting in His timing. Believing in Christ means trusting that the course will lead to the ultimate destination. Believing in Christ means sacrificing our lives for His cause rather than our cause.

Let me share with you the Parable of Peppersauce Cave. This Arizona cave has been the site where we have gone a number of years for Young Men overnight outings. The cave has some old stalactites and stalagmites that are very broken off. It is a fun place but an extremely dark and dreary place.

There is one small (narrow) entrance to the cave. Once you enter the cave and descend into it, after about 30 feet, you can no longer see the entrance to the cave.

The cave is filled with a variety of different passageways that are exciting to explore and discover. Many of these paths lead to dead ends. Many lead to places you could get stuck. Many allow you to go further into the cave.

Like any cave, when you turn off your flashlight, you can see absolutely nothing. If you were hiking this cave alone and your light (watch my word choice) went out, you would never be able to find your way out. There are too many paths, too many obstacles, too many potential falls, and too much variation in the terrain.

When you are ready to leave the cave, there is only one way out. You must find that narrow opening to exit or you will be stuck in the darkness of the cave indefinitely. Again, the only way to find the one way out is with light.

Life is a close parallel to exploring the cave. A loving God puts us down on the earth (in the cave) with a veil to prevent us from seeing everything on the other side; without the veil there would be no faith.

While in the cave, Heavenly Father desperately wants us to come back. He is very aware it is difficult to find the narrow opening in the cave to return back to Him.

This is why His light and His direction are so critical. He would never leave us without specific instructions and he would never leave us without a powerful light to find our way back

Some people claim they don't need the light, that they can find God on their own. Some people claim all the instructions are the same. This is just not true, as there are a number of paths, but only one narrow escape route. There may be a few roundabout ways to get there, but, in the end, all must leave earth or the cave through the right door in order to return to the home of God.

For each of us to find the right way, we must use the light. The light represents Jesus Christ and his detailed plan, commandments, principles, doctrines, covenants and beliefs. These things all direct us to the opening in the cave. They are the lights that lead us back to God.

When young Joseph Smith went into a grove of trees in the spring of 1820, he did not go in and start recommending paths to God. He did not go in and say, "I think the direction the Catholics are going is good, I like the Baptists' pathway because of baptism by immersion, I like the Methodists' way because their way is strict." He went it with no biases and simply asked, "Will you show me the right way back home? I just want to know your way, and I will follow that path."

God said, "I know you are sincere and so I will show you, I will lead you, I will direct you, and I inspire you; I will teach you and I will help you to establish the right way." It was never about power, honor, fame or wealth. It was always simply about the right way, the true way, God's way.

God reminded Joseph, "The right way will not be easy, it will not be comfortable, it will not be popular, it will not be without significant trials, but it will be peaceful and it will be right."

Joseph said, "Okay," and so the path has been reestablished for those desiring to know the right way, the true way, the only way back to God. I invite anyone reading this to simply ask the same question of God: "Will you show me the right way?"

He will answer you and then you will know how to get home, and he will guide you safely there, if that is the desire of your heart.

Never forget some of Alma's final words to his son, Shiblon: "*And now, my son, I have told you this that ye may learn wisdom, that ye may learn of me that there is no other way or means whereby man can be saved, only in and through Christ. Behold, he is the life and the light of the world. Behold, he is the word of truth and righteousness" (Alma 38:9).*

I love the phrase, "I feel the wind." Let me try to explain why. Wind is something you can't see, but you can see its effects. You can feel it, but you can't see it. Wind can change you and the actions you take, but you still can't see it. Wind is so much like the Holy Ghost. You can't see it, but you can feel it, you can see its effects, and it can change the way you act and who you can become.

Ask anyone who has observed the effects of a hurricane if there is power in the wind. Ask anyone who has ever felt the effects of the Holy Ghost if there is power in his influence. There is absolute power in the influence of the Holy Ghost.

The book of Ether teaches us this principle: *"And it came to pass that the Lord God caused that there should be a furious wind blow upon the face of the waters, towards the promised land; and thus, they were tossed upon the waves of the sea before the wind.*

... And it came to pass that the wind did never cease to blow towards the promised land while they were upon the waters; and thus, they were driven forth before the wind" *(Ether 6:5, 8).*

I have felt the Lord's wind blow me toward the promised land of the celestial kingdom. I have felt His influence in teaching me, shaping me, and burnishing my weaknesses. I have felt him constantly blow me in the direction of Christ and truth. I have learned that when you choose the Lord, the wind never ceases to blow in the direction of the kingdom of God.

Many members of the Church wear a CTR ring. The ring is a symbol, a reminder of who we are and of our desire to choose the right. I suggest another phrase could be used to suggest when you are on the "straight and narrow" path. The words are: Choose The Redeemer. May this ring stand as a reminder of the power of choice that you have made to follow Christ and his way.

Let me end with Nephi's powerful words: *"This is the way" (2 Nephi 31:21).*

Nephi had found the way. He had searched, he had prayed, he had received revelation and, therefore, he knew why he was here, where he was going and what he needed to do to get there. May we follow his example and do the same. May we be able to say for ourselves: "This is the way." "I have found the path. I have found the road. I have found the course. I have felt the breeze."

"And after they had been received unto baptism, and were wrought upon and cleansed by the power of the Holy Ghost, they were numbered among the people of the church of Christ; and their names were taken, that they might be remembered and nourished by the good word of God, to keep them in the right way, to keep them continually watchful unto prayer, relying alone upon the merits of Christ, who was the author and the finisher of their faith" (Moroni 6:4).

Acknowledgments

I am grateful to Cecily Condie for her diligent efforts as always on improving and revising the manuscript. I am grateful to Scott Curtis for his powerful cover designs.

I continue to be amazed and grateful for the Book of Mormon and the thousands of principles the Lord teaches us through its pages. I am also grateful for the deepened doctrines, principles of power and the greater views which the Spirit shares with me on a daily basis as I study the contents of the greatest book on Earth.

About The Author

Jeffrey "Jeff" Erickson has been a youth speaker at Especially For Youth (EFY) for over fifteen years. He has served faithfully in many capacities in the church including gospel doctrine instructor and bishop. He has a passion for writing and speaking about the gospel of Jesus Christ.

Jeff is one of the co-founders of NSFC (Non-Sunday futbol club) Arizona. This three-year old soccer club is the first non-Sunday competitive soccer club in Arizona.

He is the recent author of the powerful missionary resource <u>A Weekly Letter to Your Missionary</u>. He is also the author of the first ten books in *The Greater Views Series;* "The Fourth Nephite Effect," "The Symbolism of the Sixty," "A Voice of Thunder," "Shake the Chains of Sin,"

"Waterproofing Your Vessel," "End the Conflict of Decision," "Perfectly Honest," "An Eye of Faith," "Standing With Power," and "The Crime of Contention."

As a young man, Jeff served a full-time mission in the Canada Halifax Mission. Jeff and his amazing wife, Christine, have six sons and one daughter and reside in Gilbert, Arizona.